SUI JIANGUO

L | A | LOUVER |

VENICE, CALIFORNIA
LALOUVER.COM

SUI JIANGUO

12 September — 18 October 2014

L | A | LOUVER

VENICE, CALIFORNIA
LALOUVER.COM

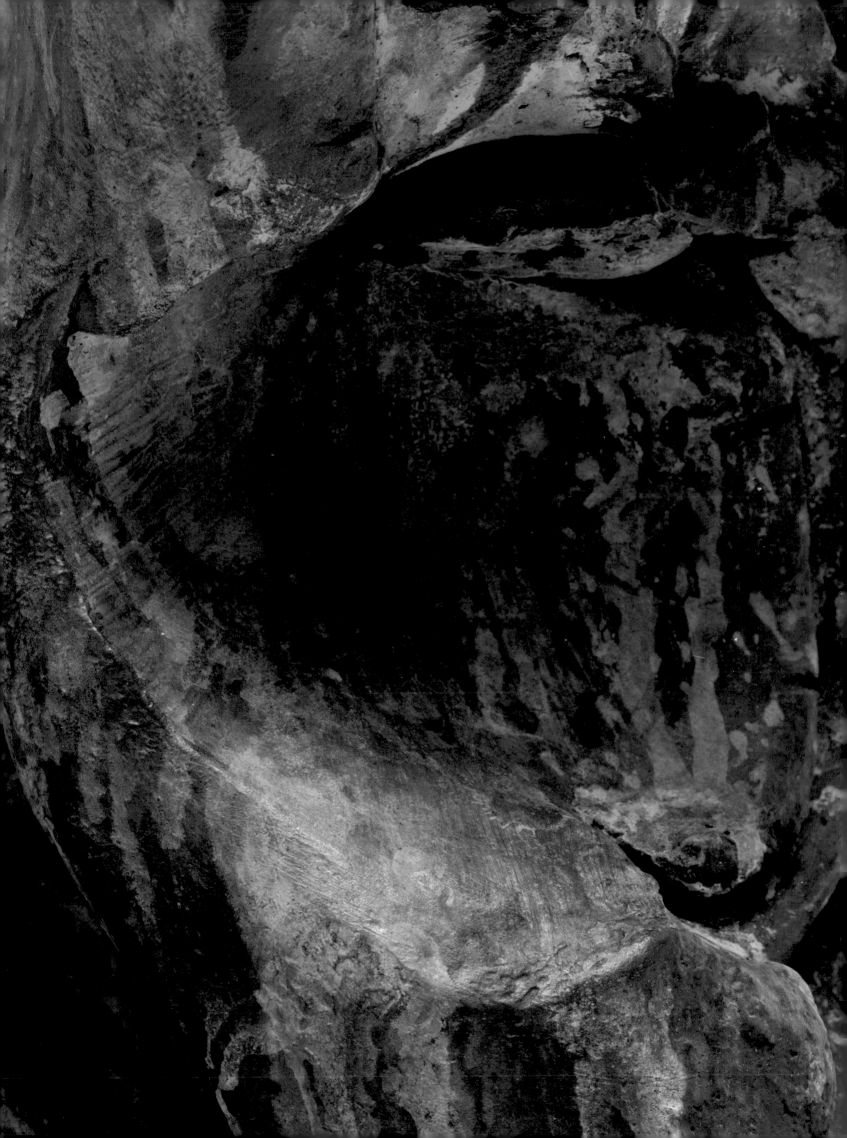

Sui Jianguo's studio, Beijing, May 2014

FOREWORD

I was introduced to the work of Sui Jianguo in 2008, and thereafter avidly researched documentation and exhibitions of his work. Four years later I had the privilege of meeting Sui here in Los Angeles, and in 2013 enjoyed an inspirational visit with him in his Beijing studio. The rich body of work in the studio, coupled with the intelligence and grace of its maker, propelled this current exhibition, Sui's first solo gallery show in the United States.

Sui Jianguo is one of the most important and influential artists working in China today. An educator as well as an artist, Sui's teaching is inextricably linked to his own artistic pursuits. As Professor and Chair of the Sculpture Department at the Central Academy of Fine Arts (CAFA), Beijing, Sui has been instrumental in addressing and enacting profound change within the Chinese arts educational system. Sui's monumental success in restructuring China's arts curriculum is adroitly articulated by art theorist Su Lei, who also contextualizes the trajectory of Sui's career alongside China's recent history in his thoughtful essay published in this catalogue.

We are also greatly honored by the eloquent text from world-renowned sculptor Richard Deacon. Richard's mastery both of his art and of the written word is unparalleled. Richard, like Sui, has a longstanding history as an educator—he has previously taught at the École Nationale Supérieure des Beaux Arts, Paris, and currently teaches at the Kunstakademie, Düsseldorf. The empathetic relationship between the two artists comes to the fore in Richard's brilliant commentary on Sui's forms and approach to making sculpture.

In addition to conveying my heartfelt thanks to both Su Lei and Richard Deacon, I am eternally grateful to Leng Lin of Pace Beijing, whose collegiate encouragement has helped make this exhibition possible. I also thank Li Jia for her invaluable assistance during the planning stages of this show. Peter Boris of Pace Gallery, with whom I have enjoyed a long-standing friendship, has provided a great deal of support and sensitivity to this project.

I am always grateful to my colleagues at L.A. Louver, especially Managing Director Lisa Jann who has displayed incredible leadership throughout all stages of this exhibition, from accompanying me to Sui's studio in Beijing, up to the final selection of works. I also thank Christina Carlos for coordinating this catalogue, which is a wonderful testament to the work of Sui Jianguo. Virginia Allison-Reinhardt and Nicoletta Beyer have provided vital research support, and Tara Hadibrata has played a key role in organizing the transport and care of Sui's sculptures. Every day I am grateful to colleagues, Christopher Pate, Kuger Peterson and Susan Yi, and fellow Directors, Kimberly Davis and Elizabeth East.

PETER GOULDS

Founding Director, L.A. Louver

August 2014

A DISCIPLE WALKING TOWARD A WORLD OF OPENNESS

At the same time, this end of an era and cultural paradigm is evidently neither the end of the world nor the end of art itself, just as the end of the age of steam engines and thermodynamics was not the end of engineering. What one discovers, on the contrary, is the proliferation of artistic forms and experiences that are not "elevated" or "refined," and that above all are not organized into a "system of arts" that falls neatly into an aesthetic field.

Yves Michaud[1]

1945	World War II ends. The last emperor's feudal reign ends in northwestern China.
1949	The People's Republic of China is established.
1966–1976	Mao Zedong launches the Great Proletarian Cultural Revolution.
1989	The Berlin Wall is torn down.
2003	Beijing's 798 Art District is named one of the world's 22 most culturally iconic city art centers by *Time Magazine*.

In the short span of 80 years, one nation's history was torn apart by foreign powers, its feudal system was destroyed, and it fell into the socialist camp during the Cold War, only to be then tossed into the multicultural system of capitalism. During this time, society was completely separated from traditional systems of organization, people's minds were repeatedly wiped clean, ideas were endlessly attacked, culture was dissected time and again, and individuals were separated from society and reorganized into new social orders. During the last 30 years, the accumulation of these changes in ideology was at its zenith. The people were not rewarded with a peaceful life for enduring these various experiments, however, and overwhelming wealth certainly did not pacify them. Instead, they marched toward their unpredictable future in a state of rootless wandering.

Amid these epic shifts, one of China's most important sculptors and conceptual artists, Sui Jianguo, represented the incredible energy released by the repeated overhaul of society. Through in-depth observation and participation in the concentrated time and space of radical social reforms, he used Chinese society as a specimen by which to represent the relationship between ideology and cultural concepts that humanity has possessed since the time of Ancient Greece. Sui also infused humanistic ideals and independent consciousness into a totalitarian system of art education, to restructure and establish a system of differentiated and plural meaning. In addition, Sui intensified interactions between diverse forms of artistic expression, helping art to cast off its reliance on authority and move toward independence, autonomy, heterogeneity and tolerance.

Sui has exhibited in international institutions, such as the San Francisco Museum of Modern Art and the British Museum. Like a lens embedded in Chinese society, the inhibitions and struggles implicit in his work testify to his pursuit of new, diverse models for coexistence, as well as his support for the resistance of intellectuals to preexisting cultural roles during the previous 50 years.

UNIFORMITY AND THE ACT OF EMBEDDING

Postmodern ideology is born in the wake of the energy crisis, like a melancholic depression formed in the aftermath of a violent loss – namely the carelessness concerning the intrinsic vitality of the world, the death of progress (technical, political, cultural) as an ideological base.

—Nicolas Bourriaud[2]

Early sketch of *Dwelling in the Fuchun Mountains* by Sui Jianguo, 1975

Sui Jianguo was born in 1956.

In early 1966, the Great Proletarian Cultural Revolution caused the government to descend into a state of anarchy, and the economy to be on the verge of collapse. While traditional culture was being thoroughly eradicated from society, the worship of individual leaders expanded uncontrollably. Universities shut down, the people lost any opportunity for an education, and a model of cultural uniformity was established. During a time of intellectual paucity and an environment of extreme political ideology, 17-year-old Sui Jianguo began studying traditional Chinese painting. Although his living conditions at the time were very modest, using a magnifying glass, Sui copied a 5 or 6 cm (2 or 2.5 in.) tall black-and-white copy of *Dwelling in the Fuchun Mountains* by Huang Gongwang

(Yuan Dynasty, 1279–1368). This traditional painting created a utopian world rich in poetic flavors, which provided a haven for Sui during the Great Purge. This all came to an end in 1976, however, with the death of Mao Zedong.

In 1978, China initiated its policy of Reform and Opening-up, carrying out economic reforms to introduce capitalist market principles. This is widely regarded as the prelude to contemporary Chinese history. On the one hand, as different schools of art started to emerge within society, artists began to reflect on the cultural consequences of the Great Proletarian Cultural Revolution. The artists also attempted to cast off the uniformity of socialist creative methods in order to adopt individualized perspectives from which to rethink reality and history. On the other hand, countless Western theories and contemporary works of art were introduced to China, sending shock waves through the artistic world. Following the rise of multiculturalism during the 1980s, society gradually abandoned the uniform standards of evaluation used during the Cold War era, former value systems started to collapse, and artists who had undergone long periods of confinement were able to release their creative enthusiasm.

Sui Jianguo personally participated in the creative enthusiasm of the 1980s and the cultural trend toward radical pluralism, including the trend's assault on uniform systems of culture. From 1980 to 1988, Sui studied at Shandong University of Arts and the Central Academy of Fine Arts (CAFA) in Beijing. He began paying close attention to the philosophy of Eastern Mysticism, particularly the principle of "Diversified Coexistence" and its emphasis on self-transformation and the mutually corresponding nature of discrete elements between individuals. At the same time, he became enamored by the idea within modern physics that a mysterious, universal energy was common to all space and matter. In a social order that makes the elements of art serve the uniform objective of politics, it is not possible to resolve the question of art itself. As a young man who had embraced such essentialist thought, Sui Jianguo yearned to find a lasting connection between the diverse elements of freedom, truth and coexistence. Throughout his life, this curiosity about relationships of coexistence within diverse systems has continuously attracted his creative energies.

BINARY ANTAGONISM AND THE ACT OF EMBEDDING

February 1989	The National Art Museum of China in Beijing holds "An Exhibition of Modern Chinese Art."
May 1989	The famous "Magiciens de la terre" exhibition is held at the Centre Georges Pompidou in Paris, prophetically proclaiming an East-West, trans-regional, cross-class dialogue.
June 1989	A series of political incidents occurs in Beijing, culminating in the freezing of all social and cultural reforms.
November 1989	The Berlin Wall is torn down, marking the end of the Cold War.

Although people reveled in the enlightened thought of the 1970s and 1980s without encountering the imagined ideological firestorm, this optimism came to a sudden halt following the 1989 political incident in Beijing. The process of society's opening up was put on hold, and the brimming enthusiasm for artistic exploration appeared feeble and weak in the face of overwhelming political power. Those groups enthusiastic about the spiritual realm and artistic reform were completely abandoned, and even artistic experiments that had received tacit government approval became unapproved expressions of the masses' wavering sentiments. Artists came to realize that contemporary art reforms were different from reforms in the economic sphere, and that art would no longer be able to circulate in government-endorsed social spaces. Consequently, art was reborn solely owing to the initiative of artists within society. Those born during the planned economy, including artists who had developed a dependency on the government, underwent an extensive weaning process. In the 1990s, these groups began moving toward two poles: one group adopted a cynical attitude as a means to resist the seriousness of traditional art, while the other group lost itself in painful reflection over the dissipated artistic enthusiasm of the 1980s.

The enthusiasm that had once burst forth became static, the once uninhibited flow of thinking was cut off, and the once natural and dynamic lives of the people were suddenly coerced into a new phase of history. These kinds of forcibly established symbiotic relationships resembled the forcing together of completely unrelated things. By using physical labor that verged on self-abuse, Sui Jianguo's *Earthly Force* series sets 30 stones, each weighing approximately 100 kilograms (220 pounds), in nets welded together from deformed steel bars. The bars then gird each stone, whereby these two incompatible materials—stone and metal—mutually reject yet enfold each other, and are forced together to form a new object.

Earthly Force, 1992, stone and welding steel, dimensions variable

Kill, 1996, rubber and nails, 25.6 x 25.6 x 25.6 in.
(65 x 65 x 65 cm)

Later, over a period of two months, Sui hammered 300,000 iron nails one by one into a 60 centimeter by 18 meter (23 inches by 59 feet) discarded rubber conveyor belt. He named the piece *Kill*. In classical Chinese, the character for the installation's name, *ji*, refers to an emperor's killing of his own subjects. The piece suggests that one's ability to endure becomes a force by which people can cause harm. The iron nails and rubber mat are embedded in each other; what was once soft is made hard, and what was originally a protective mat becomes an injurious object, existing solely because of its capacity to harm.

Through the process of embedding and being embedded, one can explore how this work of binary antagonism became the starting point for other artistic creations throughout Sui's life. Yet the result of such an antagonism is not the return of those objects to their original form, and is instead the generation of new objects. As before, there is movement from one kind of model to another, or the blending of two models that produces a new one. It is difficult to escape a unified theory of subjectivity.

COMMUNICATION AND TRANSITIONALITY

Art is a state of encounter.

—Nicolas Bourriaud[3]

During the Cold War, ideology dictated a cultural policy that forced individuals to inhabit specific cultural models. Socialists who viewed art as a strategic tool were able to establish their own education system by imitating the form and materials employed by classical models used in Western sculpture. Concurrent with the restructuring of history, they also established a uniform, domestic model of high art in the service of socialist ideology. These kinds of transplanted art forms, such as naturalistic humanism and historical perfectionism, were endowed with an innate sense of sublimity and eternity. The new rulers of the nation borrowed these models to serve as the rationale for replacing traditional culture as the governing body and as a social glue to unite the social classes. Each individual was embedded in this system and the masses were incorporated into the Eastern model of socialism, which took the "Mao Suit" as its symbol.

Clothes Vein Studies, 1998, painted bronze, dimensions variable

Legacy Mantle, 1997, painted fiberglass, 94.5 x 63 x 35.4 in. (240 x 160 x 90 cm) each

In our daily lives, this state of transition becomes an ideological blind spot and offers the individual a modicum of freedom.

These cultural models transcend both space and time, and their exchange serves as testimony to their resistance and transition as part of an endlessly expanding ideology. Between life and death, emptiness and fullness, inner and outer, and individual and collective wills, the dying slave forever exists in a qualified and restricted state; he is permanently locked in a moment of transformation.

Starting in the 1990s, Sui Jianguo began visualizing the embedded nature of this relationship. In the series *Clothes Vein Studies*, Sui regards the Mao jacket as the classic symbol for systems of power. Abstracted from predefined roles in public culture that were established by socialist artistic realism, he sculpted a Mao jacket. Sui then juxtaposed the suit with the principal tools used to found the socialist art education system—seven classical Western sculpture forms—and used them to represent the vast undertaking of using ancient Western classical art forms to establish a socialist cultural system. In the process, he paradoxically rethinks the cultural roles humanity has worshipped since the time of Ancient Greece, and how they were manipulated in the process of founding civilization.

It is important to recognize that the artist's purpose is not to discuss the rationality of any type of cultural model. Instead, the series reveals his infatuation with the incredible energy produced by antagonisms to and transformations of them. This is represented by the coalescing, overlapping and exchange of different ideologies on the marble surface; even in the fleeting moment when the slave is on the verge of death, it experiences no discontinuity. This diversity necessitates an exchange, making the piece itself serve as the site of transition. Natural life moves between two models, as if experiencing the unceasing negation of standing between two mirrors.

Motion/Tension, 2009, steel structure, electrical machinery and steel globes, diameter of steel globes: 90.6 in. and 141.7 in. (230 cm and 360 cm)

In Sui Jianguo's 2009 large-scale installation titled *Motion/Tension*, he represents the resistance and transformation of cultural systems to shocking effect. Two large metal balls, one measuring 230 centimeters (90.6 in.) in diameter and the other 360 centimeters (141.7 in.), rolled among the spectators at the exhibition; simultaneously, the viewers were subject to the cacophonous sound of metal balls being dropped from wall-like pipes enclosing the exhibition area. Audiences were made to feel the invisible shocks and jolts implicit in the reality that surrounds them, embodying the collision of ideologies from different times and spaces.

A Man-made River, 2009, washing machine cylinder, electrical machinery, stones, 19.7 x 23.6 x 39.4 in. (50 x 60 x 100 cm)

In the same year, Sui installed the cylinder of a washing machine in the corner of a museum. Titling the work *A Man-made River*, he filled the machine with a small number of crushed stones, causing the machine to emit a monotonous, coarse sound that filled the exhibition hall. The vast expanse of the museum was turned into a space of boundless nothingness, conveying the helplessness, forbearance and struggle of life in an endless and hopeless time. He used what he learned from his own experience to reflect the experience of the masses.

DIVERSITY AND OPENNESS

At the end of the 1990s, in the wake of the rejuvenated nation's economic rise, its previously rigid superstructure was nearly overturned, and former value systems, particularly those concerning the purported purity of art, were dismantled and interrogated. From the art world's perspective, the new economic structure itself was more deeply imbricated in the process of global cultural exchange, requiring the art of various regions to respond to the question of art itself and the particularities of local history.

Freedom is based on the diversity of form. In 1997, Sui Jianguo served as the chair for the Department of Sculpture at the Central Academy of Fine Arts in Beijing and convened a meeting of domestic avant-garde artists with the aim of formulating a new program for art education. The main tenets of the reforms promoted modern themes, such as the spontaneous creation of art and the symbolic meaning of different mediums, to replace socialist themes and the academic training of only certain techniques. Beginning in 2001, these far-reaching reforms and improvements to the socialist art system were gradually implemented in ten of China's major fine arts institutes, and later expanded to the entire art education system. This directly resulted in the collapse of previous aesthetic and value systems. The reforms not only established a system of schematized and differentiated meaning within the ideological structure, but also separated art from its previous location in the heart of the political system. The purpose of art will never again be forced to describe a socialist utopia or preconceived historical reforms. Instead, its purpose has become how to use art to build a new kind of reality and new modes of communication. Once art is no longer an expensive ornament decorating structures of power, and artists' works are no longer bound to a single theme, art will then cast off its role of serving others and separate itself from those systems of power. The independence and autonomy of art will allow it to reveal its own distinguishing qualities and serve as a record of the times.

Having experienced the Great Proletarian Cultural Revolution and the return of the systematization of art, Sui Jianguo believes even more strongly that the restructuring of the art system and improvement of art itself requires the dual forces of latent potential in matter and the primitive impulses of individuals. It is only with the support of these universal principles that the vitality of the individual can continue to grow strong. In his *Blind Portrait* series, Sui covered his eyes, eliminating all visual elements that might interfere with his state of mind, and he began to sculpt in clay. Allowing his body and the clay to interact with each other in their natural states, they left marks on one another. The clay that preserved the traces of the artist's body and hands was then enlarged ten to twenty times, and the latent energy possessed within the matter was released from the surface of the sculpture. The surface of the clay collected the energy of each detail, abandoning previous aesthetic forms and their attending models.

Left: *Blind Person*, 2013, 7 x 3.9 x 20 in. (18 x 10 x 51 cm)
Right: *Blind Portrait*, 2008, clay, reinforced steel bars, 98.4 x 98.4 x 267.7 in. (250 x 250 x 680 cm)

The theory of "Diversified Coexistence," which has been an ongoing influence on Sui, has gradually transformed him into an idealist in search of a rooted basis for coexistence. Sui's idealized society may remind people of Deleuze and Guattari's theory of the rhizome in *A Thousand Plateaus: Capitalism and*

Schizophrenia, in which they discuss their thoughts about symbiosis between dissimilar organisms. Regarded as an artist that is deeply embedded in the Chinese social order, Sui Jianguo has worked to separate art from systems of power, bring an end to an era of uniformity, and advance the independence and autonomy of art. By injecting humanism into the structures of communication, he has also infused those individuals just now entering this pluralistic era with a new motivating force. This notion of "Diversified Coexistence," however, implies the artist's ardent desire to advance social pluralism and a hybridized development. What is the motivating power capable of realizing the "artistic system" behind this idea? It is the principle of "eternal openness;" meaning will never again be forcibly grafted onto culture; clay need not adhere to preexisting models; the art world will be built by the direct participation of each indivudual; the principles of truth and openness will bravely give rise to a bold and daring accumulation of culture. This will be a world in flux, free from the fetters of previous form, and composed of the eternal openness of individual experience.

SU LEI | August 2014, Beijing

Su Lei is an artist, curator and art theorist. He currently teaches at Peking University, Beijing and Paris Institute of Political Studies. Su Lei lives and works in Beijing, Paris and New York.

[1] "Dans la même temps, cette fin d'une époque et d'un paradigme culturel n'est, à l'évidence, ni la fin du monde ni la fin l'art tout court. Autant assimiler la fin l'âge de la machine à vapeur et de la thermodynamique à la fin de la technique tout court. Ce que nous constatons, au contraire, c'est la prolifération de formes et d'expériences artistiques qui pour n'en être pas 'hautes,' 'raffinées' et surtout pas organisées en un 'système des arts' relèvent bel et bien du champ esthétique." Michaud, Yves. *Critères Esthétiques et Jugement de Goût*. Paris: Hachette, 2005: 9–10. Print.

[2] "L'idéologie postmoderne nait dans le sillage de la crise énergétique, telle une dépression mélancolique forme le contrecoup d'une perte brutale —en l'occurrence celle de l'insouciance quant à la vitalité intrinsèque du monde, la mort du progrès, (technique, politique, culturel) comme base idéologique." Bourriaud, Nicolas. *Radicant*. Paris: Editions Denoël, 2009: 210. Print.

[3] Bourriaud, Nicolas. *Relational Aesthetics*. Dijon, France: Les Presses du Réel, 1998: 18. Print.

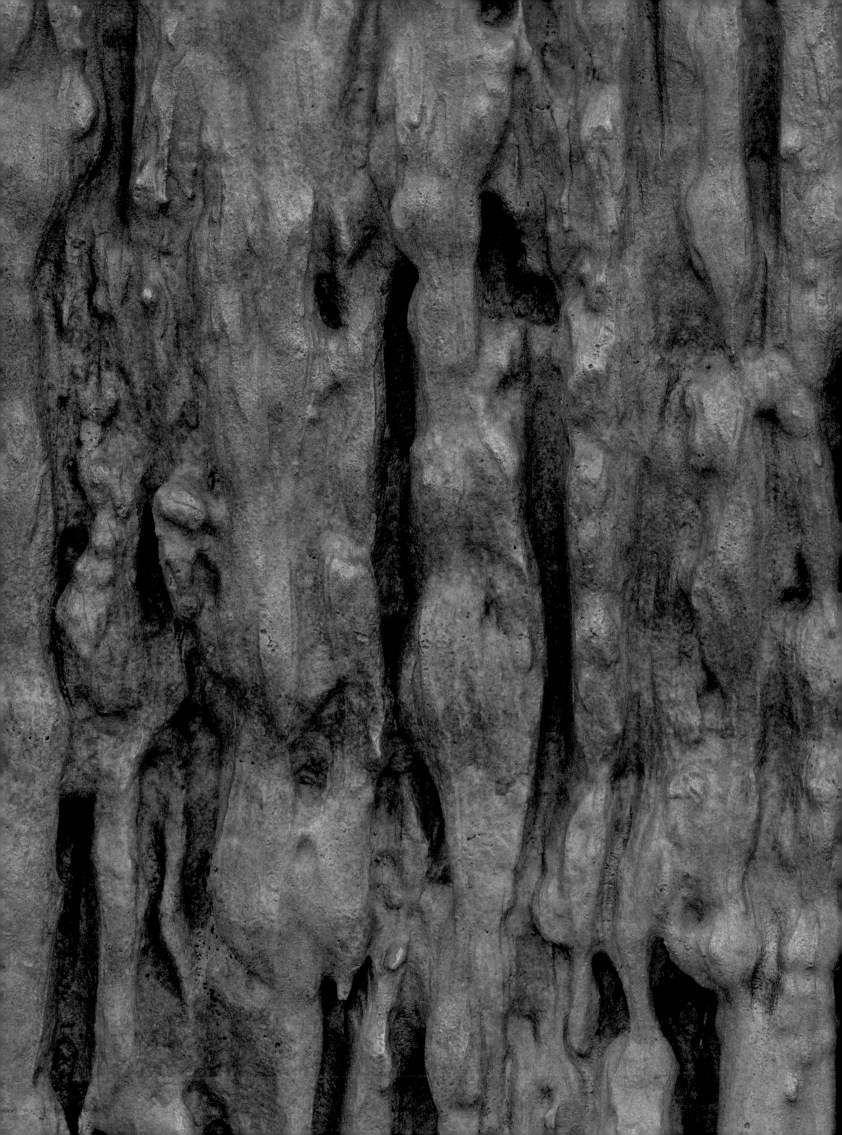

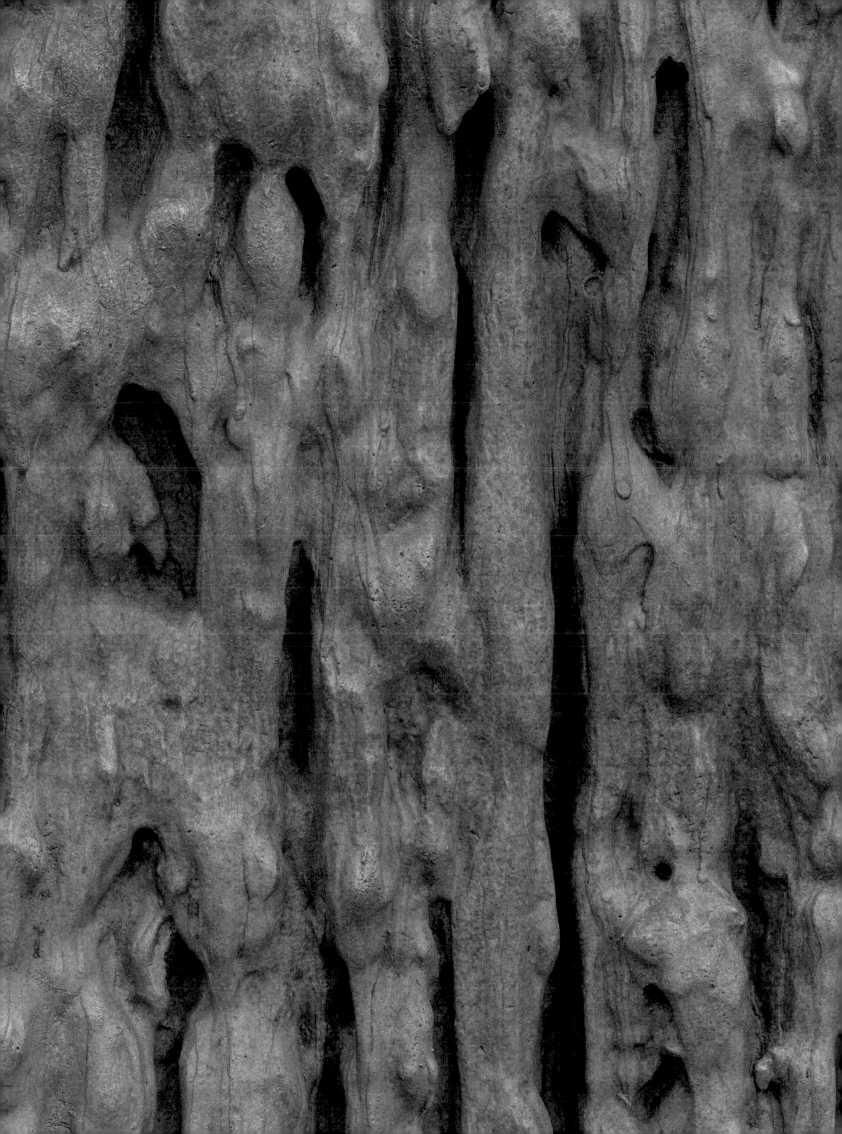

RIGHT HAND, 2008 | bronze, 78¾ x 19⅝ x 15¾ in. (200 x 50 x 40 cm)

THE BLIND #9, 2014 | cast aluminum, 22 ³/₈ x 21 ⁵/₈ x 19 ¾ in. (57 x 55 x 50 cm)

THE BLIND #8, 2014 | bronze, 23 ⁵/₈ x 19 ¾ x 19 ¾ in. (60 x 50 x 50 cm)

THE BLIND #8, 2014, *detail*

24   **BOUND SLAVE, 1998** | painted cast bronze, 90 ½ x 31 ½ x 23 ½ in. (230 x 80 x 60 cm)

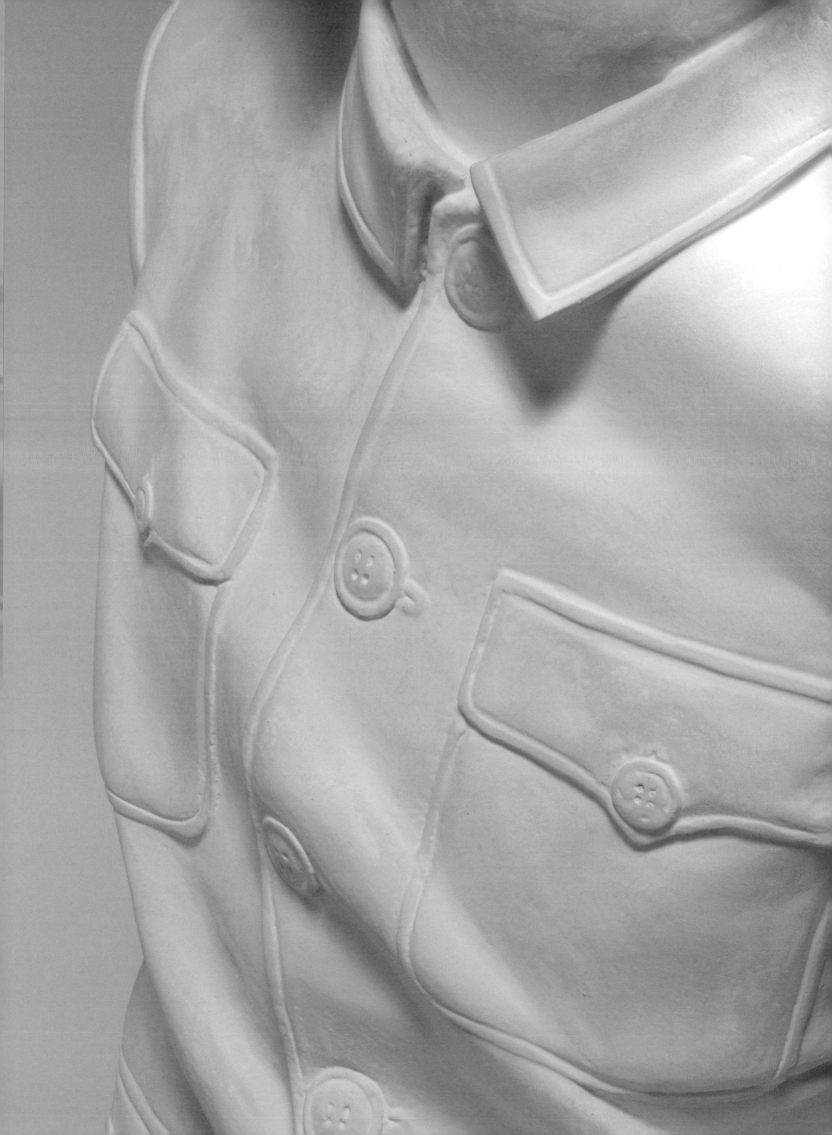

HOLLY, 2014 | bronze, 59 x 35 x 65 in. (149.9 x 88.9 x 165.1 cm)

SCHWARZWALD, 2014 | bronze, 93 x 199 x 80 in. (236.2 x 505.5 x 203.2 cm)

THE BLIND #15, 2014 | bronze, 35⅜ x 15⅜ x 19¾ in. (90 x 40 x 50 cm)

THE BLIND #16, 2014 | bronze, 12 ½ x 37 ½ x 19 ⅝ in. (32 x 95 x 50 cm)

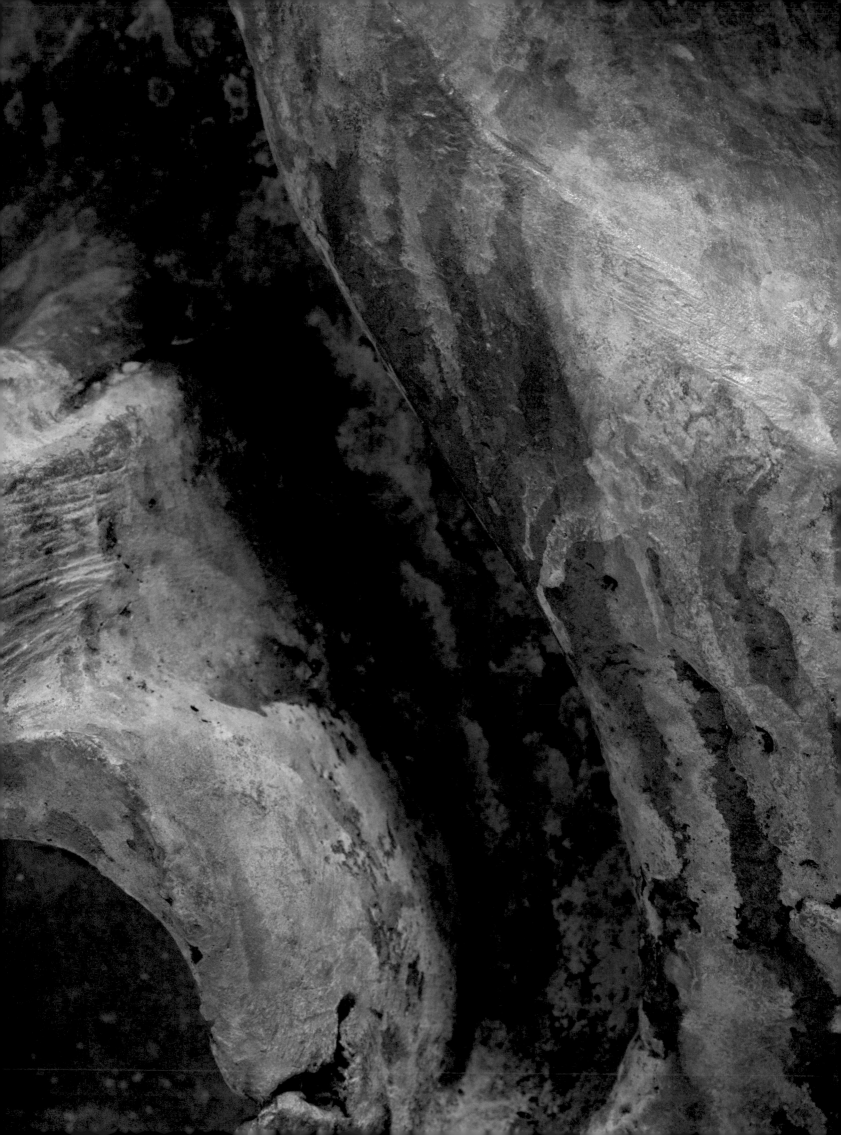

THE BLIND #13, 2014 | bronze, 25 ⅝ x 35 ½ x 17 ¾ in. (65 x 90 x 45 cm)

THE BLIND #12, 2014 | bronze, 31 ½ x 43 ¼ x 27 ½ in. (80 x 110 x 70 cm)

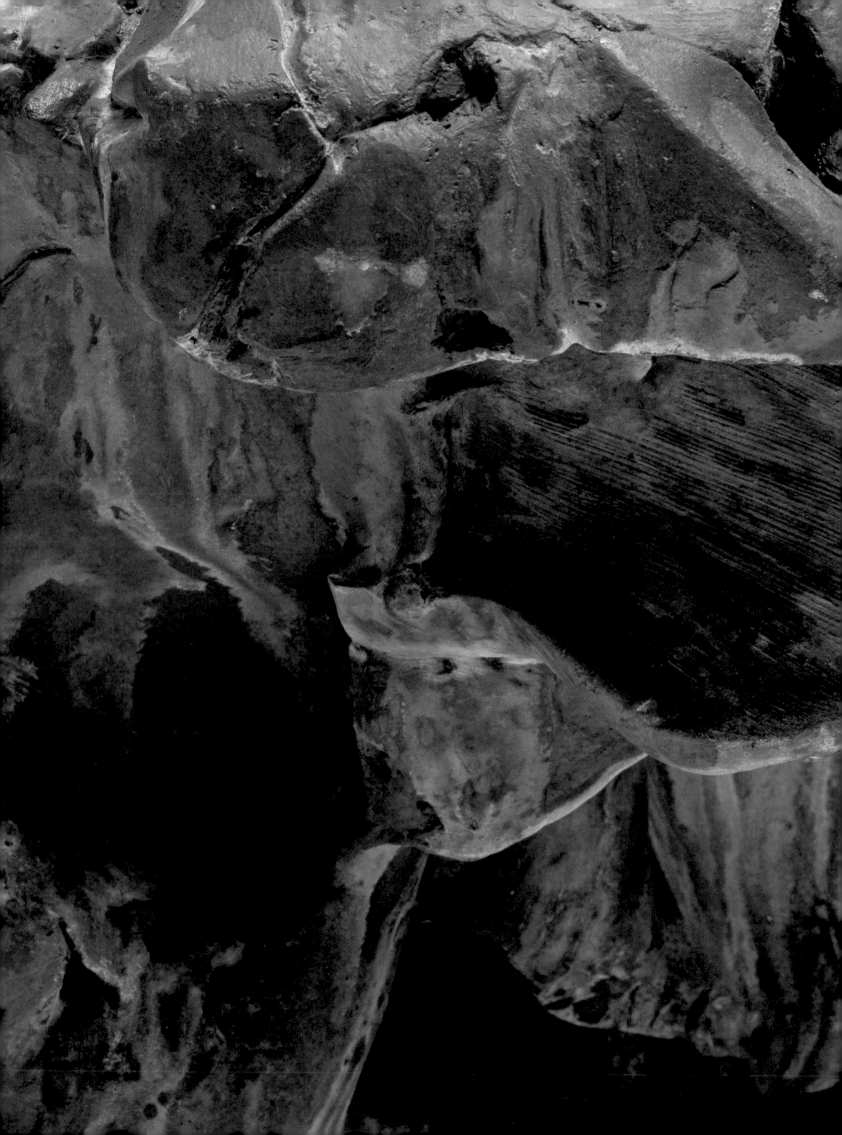

Right Hand, 2003
bronze
78 ¾ x 19 ⅝ 5/8 x 15 ¾ in. (200 x 50 x 40 cm)
Edition of 3

The Blind #9, 2014
cast aluminum
22 ⅜ x 21 ⅝ x 19 ¾ in. (57 x 55 x 50 cm)
Unique

The Blind #8, 2014
bronze
23 ⅝ x 19 ¾ x 19 ¾ in. (60 x 50 x 50 cm)
Unique

Bound Slave, 1998
painted cast bronze
90 ½ x 31 ½ x 23 ½ in. (230 x 80 x 60 cm)
Edition of 6

Holly, 2014
bronze
59 x 35 x 65 in. (149.9 x 88.9 x 165.1 cm)
Edition of 2

Schwarzwald, 2014
bronze
93 x 199 x 80 in. (236.2 x 505.5 x 203.2 cm)
Unique

The Blind #15, 2014
bronze
35 ⅜ x 15 ⅜ x 19 ¾ in. (90 x 40 x 50 cm)
Edition of 3

The Blind #16, 2014
bronze
12 ½ x 37 ½ x 19 ⅝ in. (32 x 95 x 50 cm)
Edition of 3

The Blind #14, 2014
bronze
35 ⅜ x 11 ¾ x 15 ¾ in. (90 x 30 x 40 cm)
Edition of 3

The Blind #13, 2014
bronze
25 ⅝ x 35 ½ x 17 ¾ in. (65 x 90 x 45 cm)
Edition of 3

The Blind #12, 2014
bronze
31 ½ x 43 ¼ x 27 ½ in. (80 x 110 x 70 cm)
Edition of 3

CHANGING THE SUBJECT:
THE SCULPTURE OF SUI JIANGUO

Sculpture matters to Sui Jianguo, and he has invested a great deal of his prodigious intellectual and physical energy in advancing his understanding of both what it means to make sculpture and what the subject is— in political, social, cultural, economic and experiential terms. He has been willing to periodically upend all that he has learnt and to operate with new sets of principles, although carrying forward into changed circumstances his accumulated technical knowledge. He doesn't pretend to start again as a beginner. His approach has been determinedly materialistic, combined with a quite remarkable transparency or lack of ego in his subjectivity, both at a compositional and at a mark-making level (as if he were a kind of pure transmitter of the task). The rich consequence is that expressiveness does not get in the way of expression. Psychology is not excluded, and biographic circumstances may prompt changes, but do not determine the result. "The so-called biographical aspect prompts the psychological intent of the art work," as Sui Jianguo put it in an interview with Liu Ding.[1]

Object 1, 2008, steel frame, mud, 98.4 x 98.4 x 267.7 in. (250 x 250 x 680 cm)

Left: Sui Jianguo in the studio. Right: *Blind Portrait*, 2008 installation at JoyArt, Beijing

In 2008, Sui Jianguo began the process that led to the monumental work *Blind Portrait*, which together with the accompanying *Object 1* and *Object 2* similarly produced, formed his 2008 exhibition *Revealing Traces* at JoyArt in Beijing. This exhibition initiated a group of sculptures where the imprint of a physical action—its trace—is integral to the completed sculpture. The production of that trace has been constrained in various ways—most obviously by the use of a blindfold, but also by which part of his body the artist uses in modelling the initial form. One consequence of the constraint is the muffling of, or detachment from, subjectivity in the process.

Not being able to see what you are doing makes things difficult and makes it hard to express yourself on the one hand, but equally hard to be objective on the other. It is these "blind" works that I want to focus on. Since sight is such a dominant sense, its absence, whether actual or metaphorical, engenders multiple different possibilities for meaning, many of which hinge on questions of subjectivity and of the absence of intent.

To take an example from somewhere else to illustrate the point, during the 2012 Olympics in London, there was considerable surprise, and some consternation, when it was revealed in the press that Im Dong Hyun, a champion archer on the South Korean team, was severely visually impaired. (Some said he was functionally blind, although Im Dong denies this, saying if that were the case, he would be compelled to take part in the Paralympics.) Alison Williamson of the British women's team eloquently corrected the misapprehension—seeing clearly is not so important, she said. In fact, seeing the target too clearly can cause the muscles to tense and for the archer to over-aim, trying to direct the arrow towards a precise spot on the target, disrupting the action and interfering with a smooth release. Im Dong Hyun only knows where he wants the arrow to go, and releases it in a smooth, unforced action. As he says, "For me, seeing the target and not seeing the target doesn't make any difference."[2]

Motion/Tension, 2009 installation at Today Art Museum, Beijing

A parallel phenomenon is well-known in control systems engineering (and was first corrected by the governors on steam engines). If a performance target is too accurately or precisely defined, the apparatus will oscillate with potentially disastrous rapidity around the control—off/on/off/on, etc.— a feedback loop. The behavior, known as hunting, can cause errors to amplify and the system to self-destruct. The engineering solution is to damp the system, reducing oscillation and returning the system to equilibrium in the most efficient way. Im Dong Hyun's disability damps his performance, creating a smoother action and more predictable set of outcomes.

Or to take another extended example, in clinical research, the gold standard for drug testing is the double-blind trial, whereby neither physician nor the patient know whether or not the drug being administered is under test or a placebo. The purpose of such testing is to remove, as far as possible, subjective bias from the test results. In many ways, this is equivalent to the blindfolded figure of justice, the representation of judicial impartiality and of equality before the law. In both of these examples, a part of the message seems to be that subjectivity interferes with performance. Seers and prophets are often also blind, whether in fact or as a consequence of induced trance. Blindness is understood to absent their subjectivity from entrapment in the present and to permit the emergence of foresight.

When Sui starts with the clay blindfolded, and with perhaps other constraints on his capacities, although he has a quantity in mind, and an attitude, "being blind" takes away something of his skill and knowledge. *Blind Portrait*, as a title, has many different kinds of meaning. The first is a description of the process—the artist is blind but is making a portrait, so what we see is a portrait of an unseen person. Paradoxically, it is very unclear where the face is in this work; it is up to the viewer to locate it, to bring a face to the portrait we see. However, the portrait itself can be blind—we can see it, but it cannot see us. A portrait also implies someone or something particular—the work is a portrait, a record or trace, of a blind action. The first model, produced by Sui Jianguo, becomes subject to a process of mechanical enlargement. First, a mould is made of that original which permits an identical cast, a copy, to be made. This copy is then sliced to provide sectional information, and particular surface points are identified from which a network of point measurements is taken. With this body of data, a scaled-up form is produced by applying plastic clay over a skeletal wooden armature. Using clay allows for a very faithful transcription of the original surface. A piece mould is then made from this enlarged positive from which a second wax positive, in parts, is cast. These wax parts are then invested, burnt out, and molten bronze poured into the resulting space. The final step is the cleaning up and reassembly by welding of these bronze parts, surface treatment and patination. This is a very traditional and highly crafted process involving a great deal of skilled and often arduous work. Sui Jianguo refers to it as a system—"the enlarger"—and suggests that it is the productive labour involved that mediates the transition of the blindly produced (but skillfully executed) original from the private to the public realm, and is the means or channel by which the artwork enters the distributive system of the art world. Enlargement is a manifestation of power, and is thus an economic activity embedded within the cultural context. "How capital and profit are distributed and gained—these are the goals of this 'enlarger.'"[3]

In 2009, Sui Jianguo made the extraordinary installation *Motion/Tension* at the Today Art Museum in Beijing. Two huge steel balls, one slightly smaller than the other but both threateningly large (a kind of couple or pair), rolled around the gallery space seemingly under their own volition, occasionally crashing into each other, with no concern for the viewers sheltering under the scaffolding arcade that ran round the tall atrium gallery and which blocked the path of the juggernauts. At the same time, smaller solid steel balls were raised up a vertical lift and

Chinese scholar rock in Sui Jianguo's studio courtyard, Beijing

dropped into a hopper feeding into a steel pipe running around the gallery space. The pipe even exited the building at one point, coming back in at a different location. The outlet of this pipe deposited the ball at the beginning of the vertical lift so that its journey could begin again. On their descent, the balls rattled, clattered and banged loudly through the pipe, making the space seem to shudder from this audio onslaught. All the while, the space itself was being reconfigured by the blind stumblings of the giant balls on the floor. This was a radical inversion of object/subject relations. The audience, normally itinerant in relation to sculpture, shifting individual perspective and viewpoint, was defensive, getting out of the way, subject to circumstance and sensorially bombarded. As a viewer, you were on guard and aware of something unseen, the surrounding space being manifested as it was reconfigured. The apparently fixed boundaries, the gallery walls, were buffeted by the clanging balls as they noisily made their repeated descents from top to bottom. It was as if the sculptures were themselves constructing and deconstructing their own meanings. Just as *Blind Portrait* jolts us into seeing, so *Motion/Tension* jolted us into awareness of ourselves and of our own physical being.

There is a superficial similarity between the *Blind Trace* works of Sui Jianguo and Chinese scholar's rocks. My understanding of these marvellous objects is that they are untouched (in theory), and that natural forces do the work on them—water, wind, sun, frost, etc. What human agency adds is recognition. [It's a bit less clear with regard to the bottom, which I think is sometimes modified or made flat so that the rock stands, either on a purpose-made base or table or outside (as in the garden of the Forbidden Palace)]. So there is no intentionality involved in the making, it's a question of, at first, being able to see them—they are wild in a very pure sense. However, what is implied in this recognition is that of a particular rock's capacity to capture imagination, both to represent nature and to be a microcosm through which the world emerges. And perhaps this is the point, where the superficial similarity becomes something deeper, that the *Blind Trace* works of Sui Jianguo are a microcosm through which a world emerges.

"I think it is not actually made by me alone, but is the fruit of my collaboration with God. Why (do) I think so? I had a lot of training about sculpture and I also teach the undergraduate and postgraduate students every day, therefore to shape a person, an object or something abstract is very easy. Nevertheless all these things are not what I want. I am wondering whether they can be automatically transformed into sculptures. Maybe I need to forget all (the) things I have learned." [4]

Following on from his 2005 solo show at the Asian Art Museum in San Francisco, Sui Jianguo's exhibition at L.A. Louver is his first in a gallery in the U.S. He is an artist whose work I like very much. He has made a profound and extraordinary contribution to the development of contemporary art in China through his activities both as a teacher at the Central Academy of Fine Arts in Beijing and as a highly visible artist. It has been a privilege and deeply pleasurable for me to be given the opportunity to articulate some thoughts about a complex and exemplary body of work that stretches back to the early '90s. Sui Jianguo changes the subject, and for that I am grateful.

RICHARD DEACON | July 2014

Richard Deacon (b. 1949, Bangor, Wales) is a sculptor. He has exhibited widely and internationally over the past 30 years. A major retrospective of his work, *The Missing Part*, was shown at museums in France and Germany in 2010-11, and a large-scale survey was exhibited at Tate Britain in early 2014. That same year, a collected edition of his writings, *So, If, And, But* was published in English and in German. *Richard Deacon—In Between*, a feature length film by Claudia Schmid, was also released in 2014. Recent public works have been installed in Singapore (*Upper Strut*, 2011, commissioned by Louis Vuitton), London (*Piccadilly*, 2013, in collaboration with Eric Parry), Winterthur, Switzerland (*Footfall*, 2013, commissioned by Friends of Winterthur Museum) and Gjøvik, Norway (*Gripping*, 2014, commissioned by Sparebankstiftelsen DNB). He is Professor at the Kunstakademie, in Düsseldorf.

[1] Liu Ding. "Sui Jianguo." *Sui Jianguo: Revealing Traces*. Beijing: Joyart, 2008: 42. Print.

[2] Rutherford, Peter. "In the Land of Archery, the 'Blind Man' is King." *Reuters*. Thomson Reuters, 14 Aug. 2008. Web. 21 July 2014.

[3] Liu Ding. "Sui Jianguo." *Sui Jianguo: Revealing Traces*. Beijing: Joyart, 2008: 46. Print.

[4] Sui Jianguo, et al. *Sui Jianguo: Solo Exhibition Scene Record*. Beijing: trackART, 2012: 60. Print.

BIOGRAPHY

1956 Born in Qingdao, China
Lives and works in Beijing, China

Education
1984 Bachelor of Fine Arts, Shandong University, Jinan, China
1989 Master of Fine Arts, Department of Sculpture, Central Academy of Fine Arts, Beijing, China
1989 to present Teacher, Department of Sculpture, Central Academy of Fine Arts, Beijing, China
1997–2009 Professor and Head of the Department of Sculpture, Central Academy of Fine Arts, Beijing, China

Solo and Group
Exhibitions

1986 *Exhibition of Young Artists in Shandong*, Jinan, China

Balance, 1988
gypsum, plaster
and furniture
31.5 x 35.4 x 35.4 in.
(80 x 90 x 90 cm)

1990 *Exhibition of Art Workshop No. 1,* CAFA Gallery, Beijing, China

1992 *Contemporary Young Sculptors*, National Academy of Fine Arts,
　　　　　Hangzhou, China
Position '92, CAFA Gallery, Beijing, China
20th Century China, National Art Museum of China, Beijing, China

Portraits, 1989
mixed media,
gypsum and gauze
15.7 x 9.8 x 9.8 in.
(40 x 25 x 25 cm)

1993 *Sui Jianguo and Wang Keping Sculpture Exhibition*,
　　　　　Chinese Modern Art Center, Osaka, Japan
China's New Art Post 1989, Hong Kong Art Center,
　　　　　Hong Kong, China
Cross-Strait Sculpture Exhibition, Yanhuang Art Museum, Beijing, China;
　　　　　traveled to Kaohsiung Museum of Fine Arts, Taiwan

Untitled, 1990
stone and iron cage
15.7 x 15.7 x 15.7 in.
(40 x 40 x 40 cm)

1994 *Exhibition of Works by Sui Jianguo*, Hanart Gallery, Taipei, Taiwan
Remembrance of Space, CAFA Gallery, Beijing, China
*Substance and Creativity: Asian Arts and Craft from
　　　　　Its Origin to the Present Day,* Hiroshima, Japan

Interstructure #5, 1991
stone and iron
29.5 in. (75 cm) height

1995 *Deposit and Fault*, New Delhi Culture Center, New Delhi, India
Women Site, Beijing Contemporary Art Gallery, Beijing, China
Plan for Development, CAFA Gallery, Beijing, China
From the Middle Kingdom—Chinese Avant-garde Art Since 1979,
　　　　　Centre d'Art Santa Monica, Barcelona, Spain

Deposition of Memory, 1992
stone and bamboo cage
27.6 in. (70 cm) height

1996

Exhibition of Works by Sui Jianguo, Hanart Gallery,
    Hong Kong, China
First Academic Exhibition of Chinese Contemporary Artists,
    Hong Kong Art Center, Hong Kong, China
Reality, Present, and Future: Chinese Contemporary Art,
    Beijing International Art Museum, Beijing, China
From the East of Asia: Installation & Painting, Kodama Gallery,
    Osaka, Japan
Works Nominated by Art Critics (Sculpture and Installation)
    in Jiangsu Monthly Magazine, Beijing, China
Academic Invitational Exhibition of Contemporary Art, National Art
    Museum of China, Beijing, China

Deposited Memory, 1994
stone, cement and cage
25.6 in. (65 cm) height

Earthly Force, 1992–1994
stone and welding steel
Dimensions variable

1997

You Meet the Shadow of Hundred Years, Victoria College of the
    Arts, Melbourne, Australia
Dream of China—Chinese Contemporary Art, Yan Huang Art
    Museum, Beijing, China
Continue—Five Sculptors' Exhibition, CAFA Gallery, Beijing, China
Sui Jianguo & Li Gang: Contemporary Chinese Sculpture,
    Red Gate Gallery, Beijing, China
A Point of Contact—Korean, Chinese and Japanese Contemporary
    Art, Daegu Culture and Arts Center, Daegu, South Korea

Kill, 1996
rubber and nails
25.6 x 25.6 x 25.6 in.
(65 x 65 x 65 cm)

Legacy Mantle No. 1, 1997
cast aluminum
15.7 in. (40 cm) height

1998

Personal Touch—Chinese Contemporary Art, TEDA Contemporary
    Art Museum, Tianjin, China
First Annual Contemporary Sculpture Exhibition,
    He Xiangning Art Museum, Shenzhen, China
Im Spiegel der Eigenen Tradition—Contemporary Chinese Art,
    German Embassy, Beijing, China
A Revelation of 20 Years Contemporary Chinese Art, Forbidden
    City, Beijing, China
Life: The Persistence of Memories and Drive for the Future,
    Wan Fung Art Gallery, Beijing, China

Legacy Mantle, 1997
painted fiberglass
94.5 x 63 x 35.4 in.
(240 x 160 x 90 cm)

1999

Clothes Vein Studies, Passage Gallery, Beijing, China
Second Annual Contemporary Sculpture Exhibition,
    He Xiangning Art Museum, Shenzhen, China
Gate of the Century, Chengdu Art Museum, Chengdu, China
Avant-garde in China, Galerie Loft, Paris, France
Les Champs de la Sculpture 2000, Champs-Elysèes,
    Paris, France
The Fourteenth International Asia Art Exhibition, Asia Art
    Museum, Fukuoka, Japan
Volume and Form—Singapore Art Festival, Singapore Art
    Museum, Singapore
Four Artists, Beijing Art Warehouse, Beijing, China
Departure From China, Beijing Design Museum, Beijing, China
China 1999, Limn Gallery, San Francisco, CA
Transience: Chinese Art at the End of the Twentieth Century,
    David and Alfred Smart Museum of Art, University
    of Chicago, Chicago, IL
Contemporary Art Exhibition of China, Limn Gallery, San Francisco, CA

Clothes Vein Studies, 1998
painted bronze
dimensions variable

Clothes Vein Studies,
Discobolus, 1998
painted bronze
67.7 in. (172 cm) height

2000

Shanghai Spirit—Shanghai Biennale, Shanghai Art Museum,
    Shanghai, China
Sui Jianguo and Zhan Wang, Galerie Loft, Paris, France
Sharing Exoticisms—Contemporary Art Lyon Biennale, Lyon, France
Chinese Contemporary Sculpture Invitational Exhibition,
    Qingdao Sculpture Museum, Qingdao, China
Documentation of Chinese Avant-Garde Artists in 90s, Fukuoka
Asian Art Museum, Fukuoka, Japan

2001

Transplantation In Situ, He Xiangning Art Museum, Shenzhen, China
Dream 2001—Contemporary Chinese Art Exhibition,
    Red Mansion, London, UK
Forever, Canadian Embassy, Beijing, China
Open 2001–Fourth International Sculpture and Installation, Venice, Italy
Art on the Beach, Nice, France
*Between Earth and Heaven: New Classical Movements in the
    Art of Today*, Museum Of Modern Art, Ostend, Belgium
Art and Science, National Art Museum of China, Beijing, China

2002

Paris—Pékin, Palace Cardin, Paris, France
Mirage, Suzhou Art Museum, Suzhou, China
1st Guangzhou Triennial, Guangdong Art Museum,
    Guangzhou, China
Beijing Afloat, B.T.A.P., Beijing, China
Made in China, Wilhelm Lehmbruck Museum, Duisburg, Germany
Triennial of Chinese Art, Guangzhou Museum, Guangzhou, China
Modernity in China—1980-2002, Fondacion Armando
Alvares Penteado (FAAP), Sao Paolo, Brazil
Artists of Ideal, Contemporary Art Center, Verona, Italy
Made By Chinese, Gallery Enrico Navara, Paris, France
Made in China, Ethan Cohen Fine Arts, New York, NY
Excess Interset, Ke Gallery, Singapore
Asia Contemporary Sculpture Exhibition, South Korea
International Expo, Seoul, South Korea

*Clothes Vein Studies,
Right Arm*, 2003
painted fiberglass
275.6 in. (700 cm) length

2003

Open the Sky: Contemporary Art Exhibition, Duolun Art Museum,
    Shanghai, China
The Sea and the Music: Modern Sculpture Exhibition,
    Xiamen Municipal Government, Xiamen, China
Left Wing, Left Bank Plaza, Beijing, China
Exhibition of Modern Ceramic Art, Fushan, China
Second Reality, Pingod Space, Beijing, China
Red Memory—Left Hand and Right Hand, 798 Art District,
    Beijing, China
Today's Chinese Art, China Shijitan Contemporary Art Centre,
    Beijing, China
Open Time, National Art Gallery, Beijing, China
Contemporary Sculpture—China Korea Japan, Osaka Museum,
    Osaka, Japan
Beaufort Triennial Contemporary Art by the Sea, Museum of
    Modern Art, Ostend, Belgium
CHINaRT: Chinese Contemporary Art, Museum of Contemporary
    Art of Rome, Rome, Italy; traveled to Ludwig Museum,
    Budapest, Hungary

Sleeping Mao, 2003
painted fiberglass
94.5 x 47.2 x 19.7 in.
(240 x 120 x 50 cm)

Sleep of Reason, 2005
painted fiberglass and
20,000 toy dinosaurs
200.7 x 277.6 x 29.5 in.
(510 x 705 x 75 cm)

Jurassic Time, 2000
painted bronze and steel
(230 x 250 x 460 cm)

2004

Now—Conceptual Estate in Shanghai, Shanghai Show Center,
    Shanghai, China
The First Nominative Exhibition of Fine Art Literature, Wuhan, China
Sculpture by the Sea, Bondi to Coogee Coastal Walk,
    Sydney, Australia
Gods Becoming Men, Frissiras Museum, Athens, Greece
What Is Art—Two Wrongs Can Make One Right, Xian Art Museum,
    Xian, China
Playing With Chi Energy, House of Shiseido, Tokyo, Japan
L'art à la Plage: France/Chine, organized by Galerie Enrico Navarra
    and Hanart TZ Gallery, Pampelonne Beach, Nice, France
Exposition des Sculptures Chinoises, Jardin Des Tuileries,
    Paris, France
*Between Past and Future: New Photography and Video
    from China*, International Center of Photography, Asia
    Society, New York, NY
Le Moine et le Démon, Lyon Contemporary Art Museum,
    Lyon, France
Busan Biennale 2004, Busan Sculpture Project, Eulsukdo
    Culture Centre, Busan, South Korea
Light As Fuck, National Museum of Contemporary Art,
    Oslo, Norway
Beyond Boundaries, Shanghai Gallery of Art, Shanghai, China
Hanart Celebration of Two Decades, Hanart Gallery, Hong Kong, China

2005

Sui Jianguo: The Sleep of Reason, Asian Art Museum,
    San Francisco, CA
Beautiful Cynicism, Arario Gallery, Beijing, China
Ten Thousands Year, Postmodern City, Beijing, China
To Each His Own, Zero-Space 798, Beijing, China
Xianfeng! Chinese Avant-garde Sculpture, Museum Beelden aan
    Zee, The Hague, Netherlands
Transportation Box, Jianwai SOHO, Beijing, China
On the Edge—Contemporary Chinese Artists Encounter the West,
    Cantor Center for Visual Arts, Stanford University,
    Stanford, CA
Between Past and Future: New Photography and Video from China,
    Seattle Art Museum, Seattle, WA
Fitment, Long March Space, Beijing, China
Transferred Landscape: Contemporary Sculpture from China,
    The Kennedy Center, Washington, D.C.

Made in China, 2005
neon light
787.4 in. (2000 cm) length

2006

City in Progress / Live from Zhang Jiang, Shanghai, China
Double—Kick Cracker, Tang Contemporary Art, Beijing, China
Susi—Future & Fantasy, Metropolitan Museum of Manila,
    Manila, The Philippines
Absolute Images, Arario Gallery, Seoul, South Korea
China Trade, International Center for Contemporary Asian Art,
    Vancouver, Canada
Jianghu, Jack Tilton Gallery, New York, NY
Between Past and Future: New Photography and Video from China,
    Haus der Kulturen der Welt, Berlin, Germany
On the Edge, Davis Museum and Culture Center, Wellesley College,
    Wellesley, MA

The Shape of Time, since 2006
paint and .05 in. (1.5mm) stainless steel wire
dimensions increase with time

2007	*Dian Xue—Sui Jianguo Art Works*, OCT Contemporary Art
	    Terminal, Shanghai, China
	Speeding up—Sui Jianguo Space Video, Arario Gallery,
	    Beijing, China
	The First Today's Documents 2007, Today Art Museum,
	    Beijing, China
	*Forms of Concepts: The Reform of Concepts of Chinese
	    Contemporary Art 1987–2007*, Hubei Art Museum,
	    Wuhan, China
	Red Hot: Asian Art Today from the Chaney Family Collection,
	    Museum of Fine Arts, Houston, TX
	*Metamorphosis: The Generation of Transformation in Chinese
	    Contemporary Art*, Tampere Art Museum, Tampere, Finland
	Fashion Accidentally, Museum of Contemporary Art, Taipei, Taiwan
	What is Monoha?, Beijing Tokyo Art Projects, Beijing, China
	Breathing, Shandong Museum, Jinan, China
	Top 10 Chinese Contemporary Sculptors, Asia Art Center,
	    Beijing, China
	Chinese Contemporary Society, The Tretyakov Gallery,
	    Moscow, Russia
	We Are Your Future, 2nd Moscow Biennale, Art Center Winzavod,
	    Moscow, Russia
	*China Onward: the Estella Collection, Chinese Contemporary Art,
	    1966–2006*, Louisiana Museum of Modern Art, Humlebæk,
	    Denmark
	*Things Rather Than: 14 Chinese Artists to Explore the True Image
	    of the Variation*, Doosan Art Center, Seoul, South Korea

My Stone of Weight, 2007
granite
15.7 x 9.4 x 11.4 in.
(40 x 24 x 29 cm)

2008	*Art Time Square—Exhibition of works by Sui Jianguo*,
	    Hong Kong, China
	Revealing Traces, Joyart, Beijing, China
	Slant Paradise, C-Space, Beijing, China
	Art and China's Revolution, Asia Society, New York, NY
	Beyond Limits—Sotheby's at Chatsworth, Chatsworth House,
	    Derbyshire, UK
	Conciliatory: Bozinan Biennalia, Bozinan Art Museum,
	    Bozinan, Poland
	Come Over, Li Space, Beijing, China
	Hanging in Sky Drifting on Surface, Linda Gallery, Beijing, China
	Reflective Asia—3rd Nanjing Triennial, Nanjing Museum,
	    Nanjing, China
	Hypallage: The Post-Modern Mode of Chinese Contemporary Art,
	    OCT Art & Design Gallery, Shenzhen, China
	*Half-Life of a Dream: Contemporary Chinese Art from the
	    Logan Collection*, San Francisco Museum of Modern Art,
	    San Francisco, CA
	Ships at Sea: Henk Visch & Sui Jianguo, C-Space, Beijing, China
	*New World Order: Contemporary Installation Art and Photography
	    from China*, Groninger Museum, Groningen, Netherlands
	Free Fall, Chen Ling Hui Contemporary Space, Beijing, China
	Crouching Paper Hidden Dragon, F2 Gallery, Caochangdi,
	    Beijing, China
	Hunting Birds, Tang Contemporary Art Center, Beijing, China
	Beijing: Athens, Contemporary Art from China, Technopolis,
	    Athens, Greece
	Our Future, Ullens Center for Contemporary Art, Beijing, China

Image documenting
the process of creating
a *Blind Portrait* model
from clay

Blind Portrait, 2008
clay, reinforced steel bars,
98.4 x 98.4 x 227.7 in.
(250 x 250 x 680 cm)

2009   *Motion/Tension: New Work by Sui Jianguo*, Today Art Museum,
                Beijing, China
            The Home Court, White Box Museum of Art, Beijing, China
            Beijing—Havana: New Contemporary Chinese Art Revolution,
                The National Museum of Fine Arts, Havana, Cuba
            I Can Believe, Star Art Museum, Beijing, China
            Embrace Suzhou: Exhibition of Chinese Contemporary Art,
                Suzhou Art Museum, Suzhou, China
            Art Changsha Biennale, Hunan Provincial Museum, Changsha, China
            A Conversation with Chicago: Contemporary Sculpture from China,
                Millennium Park, Chicago, IL
            State Legacy: Research in the Visualisation of Political History,
                Manchester Metropolitan University, Manchester, UK
            Spectacle—To Each His Own, Museum of Contemporary Art,
                Taipei, Taiwan
            *The Shape of Things: Contemporary Art Exchange Exhibition of
                China and Belgium*, Royal Museums of Fine Arts of Belgium,
                Brussels, Belgium

Wuchang, 2009
fiberglass and steel
393.7 in. (1000 cm) height

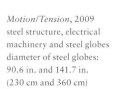

Motion/Tension, 2009
steel structure, electrical
machinery and steel globes
diameter of steel globes:
90.6 in. and 141.7 in.
(230 cm and 360 cm)

2010   *Made in China by Sui Jianguo*, Art Issue Projects, Beijing, China
            Sui Jianguo: Dream Stone, JGM Gallery, Paris, France
            Lost Utopia, MOT Arts, Taipei, Taiwan
            Made in Popland, National Museum of Contemporary Art,
                Gwacheon, South Korea
            *The City of Forking Paths, The Sculpture Project of the Expo
                Boulevard*, World Expo Shanghai 2010, Shanghai, China
            *The Constructed Dimension: 2010 Chinese Contemporary Art
                Invitational Exhibition*, National Art Museum of China,
                Beijing, China
            Sculpture: Sui Jianguo and His Students, A4 gallery, Chengdu, China
            *Zao Xing: Artwork from the Faculty of the Central Academy of Fine
                Arts*, Central Academy of Fine Arts Museum, Beijing, China
            Regulator: Today's Literature, Today Art Museum, Beijing, China
            The Property of China: Exhibition of Contemporary Art Literature,
                True Color Museum, Suzhou, China
            Meet by Chance: Project Exhibition, Joyart, Beijing, China
            Jungle: A Looking in View the Contemporary Art in China, Platform
                China, Beijing, China

Limited Moving, 2010
steel structure, electrical
machinery and steel globe
236.2 x 236.2 x 98.4 in.
(600 x 600 x 250 cm)

Dream Stone, 2010
painted corten steel
275.6 x 196.9 x 216.5 in.
(800 x 600 x 550 cm)

2011   *The Hague Under Heaven: Contemporary Sculpture from China*,
                Museum Beelden aan Zee, The Hague, The Netherlands
            Leaving Realism Behind, Pace Beijing, Beijing, China
            *Start from the Horizon: Chinese Contemporary Sculpture
                Since 1978*, Si Shang Art Museum, Beijing, China
            Ideology and Manifestation, Wenxuan Art Museum,
                Chengdu, China
            The 4th Guangzhou Triennial, Guangdong Museum of Art,
                Guandong, China
            Super-Organism: CAFAM Biennale, Beijing, China
            Collection History: China New Art, Chengdu Museum of
                Contemporary Art, Chengdu, China
            Martell Artists of the Year Exhibition, Today Art Museum, Beijing,
                China; traveled to Shanghai Art Museum, Shanghai,
                China and Guangdong Museum of Art, Guangzhou, China
            The 2nd Beijing Voice: Leaving Realism Behind, Pace Beijing, Beijing, China

Restricted Movement, 2011
steel structure, electrical
machinery and steel globe
314.9 x 98.4 x 98.4 in.
(800 x 250 x 250 cm)

Made in China, 2011
steel container
472.4 x 106.3 x 94.5 in.
(1200 x 270 x 240 cm)

2012   *Sui Jianguo's Discus Thrower*, The British Museum, London, UK
Sui Jianguo, Pace Beijing, Beijing, China
Sui Jianguo: Imprisonment and Power, Museum of Contemporary
    Arts, Singapore
Sui Jianguo: Physical Trace, Galerie Scheffel, Bad Homburg, Germany
The 7th Shenzhen Sculpture Biennale: Accidental Message,
    OCT Contemporary Art Terminal, Shenzhen, China
Kyiv Sculpture Project 2012: Special Project, Kiev, Ukraine
Sculpture 2012, Hubei Museum of Art, Wuhan, China
The Unseen, Fourth Guangzhou Triennial, Guangdong Art Museum,
    Guangzhou, China
Reactivation: 9th Shanghai Biennale, Power Station of Art,
    Shanghai, China

Punch Piece, 2011
marble
23.6 x 19.7 x 15.7 in.
(60 x 50 x 40 cm)

2013   *Sui Jianguo: Physical Trace 2*, Galerie Scheffel, Bad Homburg,
    Germany
Blickachsen 9: Sculpture in Bad Homburg and Frankfurt RheinMain,
    Frankfurt, Germany
Space Drawings, Kunsthal KAdE, Amersfoort, Netherlands

Video still from
Physical Trace, 2013

2014   *Sui Jianguo*, L.A. Louver, Venice, CA
Busan Biennale 2014, Busan Museum of Art, Busan, South Korea
Future Returns: Contemporary Art from China, Eli and Edythe Broad
    Art Museum, Michigan State University, East Lansing, MI

SELECTED READING

BOOKS/MONOGRAPHS

2004 Kelly, Jeff and Sui Jianguo. *Sui Jianguo: The Sleep of Reason*. San Francisco, CA: Asian Art Museum, 2004.

2009 Sans, Jerome. "Sui Jianguo: Made in China." *China Talks: Interviews with 32 Contemporary Artists*. Hong Kong: Timezone 8, 2009: 72–77.

2011 *Sui Jianguo*. Taipei, Taiwan: Artist Publishing (Museum of Contemporary Arts Singapore), 2011.

2012 Dal Lago, Francesca. "Looking for Form: The Sculpture of Sui Jianguo." *The Hague Under Heaven: Modern Sculptures from China*. Zwolle, The Netherlands: WBooks, 2012: 83–97.

ARTICLES

2005 Hamlin, Jesse. "Chinese artist Sui Jianguo puts Mao to rest in colorful metaphor." *San Francisco Chronicle*, 16 February 2005.

2008 Chang Tsong-zung. "A Secret Anti-Modernist: Sui Jianguo and His Retirement Project." *Yishu Journal of Contemporary Chinese Art*. Vol. 7. no. 3, May–June 2008: 10–21.

2012 Holden Platt, Kevin. "Chinese Sculptors' Exploration of Ancient Traditions Sparks Artistic Rebirth." *New York Times*, 15 March 2012.

2014 Burris, Jon. "Sui Jianguo: Discovering His Own Voice." *China Today*. Vol. 63. no. 5, May 2014: 78–79.

PHOTOGRAPHY CREDITS

Jeff McLane: cover, 24–27
Fredrik Nilsen: opposite Table of Contents, 4–5, 14–23, 28–47, 56–57
Lisa Jann: 2, 53
Inside front and back covers:
Video stills from *Physical Trace*, single screen video, 30 min.
Directed by Wang Dongshen, produced by Sui Jianguo studio, April 2013
All images of artwork © Sui Jianguo

CREDITS

© 2014 L.A. Louver and Sui Jianguo
"A Disciple Walking Toward a World of Openness" © Su Lei
"Changing the Subject: The Sculpture of Sui Jianguo" © Richard Deacon
All works by Sui Jianguo.
All rights reserved.
No part of the contents of this catalogue may be reproduced, in whole
or in part, without the permission from the published L.A. Louver.
ISBN: 978-0-9843051-8-6
Library of Congress Control Number: 2014949501
Catalogue designed by Keith Knueven and Lydia Park for Keith & Co., Los Angeles, California
Printed by Typecraft, Wood & Jones, Pasadena, California
Catalogue coordination by Christina Carlos
Edited by Christina Carlos and Lisa Jann

This catalogue was produced on the occasion of the exhibition

SUI JIANGUO

12 September — 18 October 2014

L | A | LOUVER |

VENICE, CALIFORNIA
LALOUVER.COM

L.A. Louver
45 North Venice Boulevard
Venice, California 90291
tel: 310.822.4955
fax: 310.821.7529
info@lalouver.com